Cognitive Behavioral Therapy

—————— ❧❦❧❦ ——————

How to Combat Depression, Fear, Anxiety and Worry (Happiness can be trained)

Chris S Jennings

express written consent from the Publisher. All additional right reserved.

The information in the following pages is broadly considered to be a truthful and accurate account of facts and as such any inattention, use or misuse of the information in question by the reader will render any resulting actions solely under their purview. There are no scenarios in which the publisher or the original author of this work can be in any fashion deemed liable for any hardship or damages that may befall them after undertaking information described herein.

Additionally, the information in the following pages is intended only for informational purposes and should thus be thought of as universal. As befitting its nature, it is presented without assurance regarding its prolonged validity or interim quality. Trademarks that are mentioned are done without written consent and can in no way be considered an endorsement from the trademark holder.

Your Free Gift

As a way of saying thank you for your purchase, I wanted to offer you a free bonus e-book called **3 Incredible Life Changing Daily Habits That Can Help You To Heal Any Pain In Your Life**

Download the free ebook here: https://www.subscribepage.com/healing

Are you tired of letting your negative emotions consume you? Life throws a lot of curveballs at us: illness, abandonment, death, heartbreak, injury, the list goes on. We have found 3 scientifically endorsed daily habits that can significantly help you to heal any emotional pain and help take back control for you to start living a more positive life right now.

Listen to this book for free

Do you want to be able to listen to this book whenever you want? Maybe whilst driving to work or running errands. It can be difficult nowadays to sit down and listen to a book. So I am really excited to let you know that this book is available in audio format. What's great is you can get this book for FREE as part of a 30-day audible trial. Thereafter if you don't want to stay an Audible member you can cancel, but keep the book.

Benefits of signing up to audible:

- After the trial, you get 1 free audiobook and 2 free audio originals each month
- Can roll over any unused credits
- Choose from over 425,000 + titles
- Listen anywhere with the Audible app and across multiple devices
- Keep your audiobooks forever, even if you cancel your membership

Click below to get started
Audible US - https://tinyurl.com/y5r2w7gc
Audible UK - https://tinyurl.com/yx989ccj
Audible FR - https://tinyurl.com/yy3kufez
Audible DE - https://tinyurl.com/y2sqymrr

Table of Contents

Introduction 1

Chapter 1: Understanding Depression, Fear, and Anxiety 3

Chapter 2: Setting goals and lifestyle changes..25

Chapter 3: Face Your fears, anxiety, depression, and Worry.......................................47

Chapter 4: Mindful Acceptance 67

Chapter 5: Narrowing down your specific Worries..81

Chapter 6: Blue Print for Well-being................91

Conclusion 99

Introduction

There are plenty of books on this subject on the market, thanks again for choosing this one! Every effort was made to ensure it is full of as much useful information as possible, please enjoy!

Depression and anxiety disorders depict a life driven by anxiety. It is an important part of being human. Every human being uses anxiety as a survival mechanism. It consists of a sequence of responses and reflexes which prepare us to stay out of danger. This is one of the reasons why we experience anxiety.

Most of the time it sits in the background until that point when we need it. However, for many people anxiety develops and becomes stronger for no good reason. It begins to show up frequently and in an intense manner. It can become more dominant and over time, it may result in serious problems such as unnecessary worry, panic attacks, feelings of apprehension, obsessive thoughts and compulsive behaviors.

Cognitive Behavioral Therapy

Continuous experience of anxiety, phobias, depression, and panic may leave us feeling hopeless and helpless. And there is nothing that can be done to free us from it. Years of reading books and websites, searching for what could be the answers, attempting to find ways to think, ways to behave, therapy, medication and many more can leave us feeling exhausted without a single hope and even very anxious.

And yet, many people successfully overcome all these troubles. Often after years and years of experience, experimenting and researching their problem. They discover the answer. They don't wake up one morning and find their problem is gone, no. Instead, they grow, let it go and change. Their problem vanishes when they begin to understand, build a different perspective and begin to behave differently. Each chapter of this book will help you learn different ways which you can overcome your fear, anxiety, and depression. The chapters have different step by step processes which you can follow to ensure that you combat your feelings of anxiety.

Chapter 1:
Understanding Depression, Fear, and Anxiety

Everyone has experienced depression at one point in their life. Each person's experience is different because the symptoms are not the same. Many people feel sad occasionally, or go through rough times, but they have certain areas in their life when they feel good and love specific aspects of themselves. However, this is not the same for some, life is more of a struggle. They feel sad about themselves and their lives. At times they feel completely hopeless. If you have ever felt this way, chances are that you might be depressed.

What is depression?

Most people often say "they feel depressed" to mean they are feeling sad or miserable about life. Usually, these feelings disappear after sometime. However, if the feelings are disrupting your life activity and continue to disturb you even after 2-

3 weeks, or they recur over and over again, for a few days at a time, you could be depressed.

Depression is a lengthy and persistent mood which can affect many aspects of one's life. It is characterized by feelings of sadness, loneliness, excessive guilt, and worthlessness. Other times you may even develop suicidal thoughts. A normal depression can extend for a few minutes to a few days. We have all gone through these periods of being "sad" or "down". These feelings are part of being human. But, when depression becomes extreme and goes beyond the normal periods of time, it is far from the everyday sort. For this extreme type of depression, you will need to consider getting help. There are different forms of depression:

- **Seasonal affective disorder (SAD)-** Just as the name suggests, this is a seasonal form of depression. It often appears in the winter and autumn, the time when days are short and the sun is low in the sky, and it starts to improve when the days get longer and brighter.

- **Postnatal depression-**many mothers experience the 'baby blues' immediately after giving birth to their baby, but it then disappears after 1-2 days. Postnatal depression is a more severe problem and can take place at any time either two weeks or two years after giving birth.

- **Bipolar disorder (Manic depression)-**Some people develop major mood swings when the periods of depression switch with the periods of mania. Mania is when they are in a high state of excitement and may attempt to do over-ambitious ideas and schemes. During this time, they have periods of severe depression.

- **Psychotic depression-** takes place when an individual has extreme types of depression.

- **Persistent depressive Disorder-**This is a form of depression which may extend for two years.

- **Major depression-** It is a form of depression characterized by severe symptoms that disrupt a person from working, sleeping, eating and enjoying life. An instance of major depression may occur once in a lifetime.

Symptoms and Signs that show up if you have depression

Sadness. There are certain people with depression who might not feel sad at all. Depression has many different types of symptoms, not forgetting to mention the physical symptoms. If you discover that you have any of the symptoms following lasting for more than 2 weeks, chances are that you have depression:

- Feeling of pessimism, hopelessness.

- Loss of interest participating in activities and hobbies.

- Persistent sadness, empty mood or anxiousness.

- Difficulty in making decisions, concentrating or remembering things.

- Feeling guilt, helplessness, and worthlessness.

- Continuous physical symptoms.

- A feeling of committing suicide

- Experiencing sleepless nights, oversleeping or insomnia.

- Loss of appetite and changes in weight.

- Restlessness and irritability.

- Turning to alcohol or drugs.

- Getting angry easily.

- Crying for no good reason.

Factors that contribute to Depression

Many different factors contribute to depression. It does not have a single cause. It can either be triggered or occur spontaneously without any relation to a physical illness, life crisis or other risks. Scientists have come up with various factors which they think may lead to depression:

- **Trauma.** When a person experiences trauma at an early stage, it can result in long-term changes in the way their brains respond to feelings of stress and fear. These changes in the brain can explain why people with a history of childhood trauma have a high probability of depression.

- **Genetics.** Suicide risks and mood disorders seem to run in families, however, genetic inheritance is only a single factor.

- **Life circumstances.** Financial status, marital status and the place a person is living play a certain role in determining whether a person may develop depression or not.

- **Structure of the brain.** Results from imaging studies indicate the frontal lobe of the brain becomes less active when a person feels depressed. Depression is further associated with changes in the way the pituitary gland and hypothalamus can respond to hormone stimulation.

- **Substance abuse.** Close to 30% of people who abuse drugs have depression.

- **Other medical conditions.** People who have a history of chronic pain, sleep disturbances, anxiety, attention-deficit hyperactivity disorder and medical illness are likely to have depression.

Depression doesn't care whether you are a child or a grown up, it can attack anyone at any age. However, in young children, it starts while they are in their early 20s. For the adults, anxiety disorders arise in the form of abnormal levels of anxiety. It also shows up together with a complicated medical illness like diabetes and heart diseases. Depression can worsen these conditions. In some cases, medication recommended for these illnesses may lead to side effects which cause depression.

How depression affects people

Depression affects people in many different ways. Certain symptoms might show up in a person and fail to appear in another person. Some people only experience a few symptoms of depression. Others have many symptoms. The scale of severity, the number of times the symptoms appear, and the period the symptoms are going to stay will change depending on the individual and the type of illness.

Women

Women with depression don't experience the same symptoms. However, depressed women have symptoms of guilt, sadness, and worthlessness.

Depression is prevalent amongst more women than men. Hormonal, biological, lifecycle and psychological factors are unique to women. This might be associated with their higher rate of depression. For example, most women are weak after giving birth, therefore, they are likely to suffer from postpartum depression.

Men

How men suffer from depression is very different from the ladies. Women who have depression may feel sad and worthless, men are not the same. For men, they lose interest and feel irritable. Some even have sleepless nights. Men might resort to drugs or alcohol when they feel depressed. They could also feel discouraged, frustrated, irritable, abusive and angry. There are certain men who get busy in their jobs as a mechanism to avoid speaking with their family friends about the problems which they are going through.

Children

Before they reach puberty, boys and girls have an equal chance to develop depression. Children who are feeling depressed might pretend to their parents that they are sick. Some stick to their parents while others decide not to go to school. Like men and women, the behaviors of children are also different. This means that it can be very difficult to tell if a child is suffering from depression. Other times the parent can be worried about the behavior of the child, or a teacher can notice that a child has changed in the way he or she normally behaves.

Teens

If there are difficult times for a person while growing up is when you are a teen. This is the time when you begin to develop your identity. There are a lot of issues which you seem to be at war with as a teen. Some of the main issues include sexuality and the ability to make independent decisions without external interference. Bad moods are predicted to affect a teen; however, depression might be different.

Children who are older and teens suffering from depression might sulk, be negative, irritable and find themselves in trouble at school. If you are not sure whether your teen is suffering from depression, you should measure the length of time the symptoms have persisted. Again, study the way your teen is behaving far from her normal self. They might also have a high likelihood of committing suicide.

Children and teenagers often depend on their parents, teachers, or any person that is older and mature enough to notice their suffering and help them recover from it. Many teens don't know what to do or where to seek help for mental treatment. Some have a perception that treatment won't help. Others don't seek help because they believe that the symptoms of depression are just part and parcel of the usual stress of being a teen at school. In some cases, teens feel terrified about the way the rest of the

world is going to look at them when they look for
further mental treatment.

Grownup People

Feeling depressed beyond the normal period is
not a sign of oldness. In fact, many studies show
that the older you get the more comfortable you
feel. It is not easy to identify depression in aged
people because they may not have clear
symptoms.

Some older people with depression appear tired,
have sleepless nights, or look grumpy and
irritable. Attention problems as a result of
depression might appear. Older adults could also
experience medical conditions such as cancer,
heart disease, and stroke, which might trigger
depressive symptoms. Or they might be taking
medications which have side effects that lead to
depression.

Some older adults could experience what doctors
refer to as vascular depression. This occurs when
the blood vessels in the body harden and stiffen.
Now, when the blood vessels get stiff, they acts
as a barrier in allowing the normal flow of blood
to the rest of the other body organs. Those

people who suffer from vascular depression have a high risk for stroke or heart disease.

Sometimes it becomes difficult to differentiate grief from major depression. Experiencing sorrow when your close family member passes on is a common symptom that does not need professional help. However, extended grief is not normal. It could mean the person is severely depressed. Adults growing old have a higher chance to suffer from depression especially if they once went through it while they were young.

Understanding Fear and anxiety

Fear and anxiety are something most people experience in the course of life. However, having just some anxiety is good because it can help people to get ready for challenges, difficult situations, and deal with dangers.

Fear is a powerful emotion. It has a very strong influence on your body and mind. Fear can trigger strong signals of response when we're in emergencies. For instance, if we are being attacked. Fear can also invade us when we are asked to stand and deliver a speech to a big crowd of people or about to sit for exams.

Chapter 1: Understanding Depression, Fear , and Anxiety

Anxiety is a term we use to refer to some types of fear having to do with the thought of a danger or something going wrong in the future. Fear and anxiety can occur for a short time and then disappear, but they can also extend for a longer time and you can get disturbed with them. Sometimes, fear and anxiety can take over your life, interfere with your eating cycle, travel, sleep, concentration, or even going to school or work. This can stop you from doing things that you want to do, appreciate doing, and also affect your health.

Some people are taken over by fear and want to avoid situations that may make them anxious. It can be difficult to put an end to this cycle, but there are lots of ways to do it.

However, certain forms of anxiety are common in a person's life:

- **Infants aged 18-months** have a stranger anxiety. It is a normal and common type of anxiety which many young children have when they are standing or sitting close to strangers. This makes the young children want to stay near their parents. Furthermore, this is healthy and protective for an infant to have since it helps them stay close to their parents.

- **Kids between 2-6** are petrified of monsters, darkness, and giants.

- **Kids age 7-12** are fearful of losing their parent or even bad things that could happen to them.

- **Teenagers experience** social fears of getting accepted and fitting in the complicated social life of a teenager.

When a person has so much anxiety to the point where it interferes with their normal life and prevents them from doing certain things, then it is referred to as an Anxiety Disorder or Anxiety Condition.

Symptoms of anxiety

Some of the common symptoms that people may experience when they are anxious include:

Physical sensations

- Poor concentration
- Dry mouth
- Feeling dizzy
- Diarrhea
- Low energy
- Frequent urination
- Rapid heartbeat
- Difficulty swallowing
- Pain in chest
- Discomfort in the abdomen

Emotional or Psychological symptoms

- Irritability
- Insomnia
- Feeling unreal
- Fear that you are losing it
- Difficulty concentrating

Major types of Anxiety Conditions

There are different forms of anxiety situations that people can experience:

Generalized Anxiety Disorder. A kid suffering from this form of disorder will have a hard time managing their fears, this means that they will become petrified of everything. Excessive worries lead to stress on the body. So, this type of disorder also has physical symptoms such as fatigue, irritability, difficulty concentrating, restlessness, sleep problems and muscle tension.

Obsessive Compulsive Disorder. The condition may have repetitive and distressing:

- Obsessions-thoughts or images

- Compulsions-habits that one can't resist and feels pressured to do.

A classic example of obsessions includes obsession of cleanliness, which results in a compulsion of cleaning or handwashing repetitively.

Panic disorder. These are recurrent impulsive episodes of panic that are related to physiological and psychological symptoms. Physical symptoms include breathing problems, chest pain, and dizziness. Some of the psychological and behavior symptoms consist of extreme fear, and the need to run away from the condition causing panic.

Phobias. Most people experience phobias when they are scared of a specific thing such as snakes, storms etc.

Social phobia. This is fear of social situations where the person stands before unfamiliar people. It is beyond normal shyness. It prevents people from attaining their full potential at work and school because of their behaviors to avoid school, social or work situations.

Post-traumatic stress disorder. This is a delayed reaction to a traumatic situation such as a house on fire, car accident, or being hurt by others through bullying. The person might relive the situation, and have nightmares, flashbacks or deep emotions. The person might be on edge all the time, with sleep problems and low concentration and energy.

Selective Mutism. This is the failure to speak in certain social situations such as school while speaking in other social places such as at home.

Separation anxiety disorder. It is an excessive anxiety about separation from a parent or caregiver that is not right according to the child's developmental level and age. For instance, a 2-year old getting nervous about being detached from their parent is usual, but a 7-year old with the same signs would be abnormal.

Common Anxiety Situations for Children

Some of the common triggering events for children include:

- Farewell from a loved one

- Social fears like interacting with new friends, scoring good grades and encountering with new people.

- Performance anxiety such as public speaking, speaking in front of the class, writing exams or tests.

- Academic stress from the need to get good grades.

- Worries about the things that may happen such as "What if ...."

- Teasing or bullying by others.

What do fear and anxiety feel like?

When you are frightened or extremely anxious, your mind and body operate quickly. These are some of the things that may happen:

- Fast heartbeat
- Having dry mouth
- You have a loose bowel
- You sweat a lot
- You can't concentrate on one particular thing
- You remain frozen in one place

The above things could occur because whenever your body develops a sense of fear, it begins to prepare yourself for an emergency. It is this getting ready for the emergency that results in increased blood flow around your body muscles and increased level of concentration on the thing that seems to be a threat.

With the feeling of anxiety, you may experience some of the above symptoms as well as a nagging sense of fear, and you may become irritable, experience sleep problems, develop headaches, or experience problems going to work and planning for the future.

Steps of Anxiety

The cognitive-behavioral model for anxiety has different stages:

1. Triggering event
2. Thoughts
3. Feelings
4. Behaviors

Chapter 1: Understanding Depression, Fear , and Anxiety

1. **Triggering Event.** Anxiety begins after a triggering event. For instance, a child with anxiety is waiting to see her parent after school, but the parent is delayed.

2. **Thoughts.** The next stage is the person with anxiety experiences anxiety thoughts or thoughts of worry. Often, the thoughts revolve around two major themes:

   a. A feeling of powerlessness, or

   b. The world is a threatening place

3. **Feelings.** Thoughts of anxiety result in anxiety feelings, which vary in the level of severity. We have mild worry, anxiety, then sheer panic.

4. **Behaviors**. A common practice when one is feeling anxious is to run away from the danger that makes people avoid their fears. However, running away from fear doesn't help, but only adds salt to the problem in the future.

Chapter 2:
Setting goals and lifestyle changes

Many of us have been in a state where we've set goals but then failed to accomplish them. The passion may have been present and we had the best intentions, but nothing happened. Life got busy and we forgot all about our goals. Then, as time passed by, we were reminded of our goals, we discovered that we are not closer to achieving our goals.

Goal setting in therapy, and its importance

When it comes to setting goals in therapy, one must identify some of the outcomes they want to achieve. It is important that the goals are measurable, achievable as well as observable. Furthermore, the goals must relate to the behavioral changes or cognitive changes of the present problem. Goals extend the period of sessions, allow one to perform the specific treatment. This gives time for the therapist to measure the improvements.

Cognitive behavioral therapy(CBT) consists of a goal-oriented treatment method in itself. Focused on changing the behavior, patterns of thinking, as well as the attitude one might have towards the challenges they are facing.

When it comes to setting goals, a CBT therapist might help you:

- Identify the goal
- Concentrate on the performance and not just the outcome
- Discover the difference and connection between short-term and long-term goals.
- Have goals which are said to be S.M.A.R.T goals.

Identify the goal

It is important to have your goal identified. Let's say that you have the set goal to complete a marathon. If you set a clear vision about this goal, you will:

- Understand what the goal is and why it is important to achieve it.

- What are some of the hardships that can take place?

If you work with a CBT therapist, he or she can help you concentrate on your strengths and let you gain positive attitude right from the start.

Long-term or short-term goal?

Something else that a CBT will help you is to understand the link and difference between long-term and short-term goals. If you want to participate in a marathon, it is not enough to buy running shoes and then wait for the day of the marathon to arrive. No!

When you put your focus on achieving your goals, chances are that you will achieve the outcome goal. This doesn't mean now you should forget about the main goal. The secret is to learn how to maintain your focus, and balance between the two.

Assessing Barriers, Facilitators, Importance and Confidence

Once multiple goals or a single goal has been achieved, it is important for the therapist to examine the situation of the patient and attitude about the goals. For instance, a therapist should ask for some little details of the patient's life which may act in preventing them from achieving their goal. A resilient family together with a mature social-support structure might help a patient to accomplish their goals.

An assessment of importance and confidence are also critical. A therapist should make a request to the patient to let her rate the level of importance of their or her own goal. The scale should run from 0-100. A scale of 0 should mean that the goal is not that important while a rate of 100 means the goal is very important.

The therapist should then discuss with the patient if the ratings are below 60. The patient together with the therapist must sit down and re-evaluate the goals. The therapist could ask the patient to tell him or her the level of confidence. It is good if you can give freedom to the patient to say their or her confidence in choosing the goal.

Tips to use when setting the goals

- **Explain the basis for why you need to set the goals.** By following this route, you will help the patient to develop an understanding of the treatment. Plus, it shapes the patient to have a clear view of how much commitment she needs.

- **Highlight desired results.** This consists of the therapist helping you define your goals and specify reasons for coming for the treatment.

- **Be Specific about your goal.** Perform a deep analysis of each goal. This involves discovering the objective of each goal. Guide the patient so that they may find the right path in discovering goals that they may require to modify.

- **List goals by adopting a positive trend.** This will help the patient to outline goals which they prefer to accomplish rather than what they don't want to.

- **Measure the merits and drawbacks of a goal.** This will help understand some of the negatives and positives of accomplishing this goal. In any cases, it helps in understanding the financial budget that might be involved. Furthermore, it works as an inspiration to the patient who has not yet made a decision.

- **Write down some of the behaviors linked to the goal**. This action helps the patient to see the importance of getting involved in a given activity. To help the patient have a chance to succeed, it is important to define goals which are possible to achieve. Don't try to do only one thing daily. This makes everything hard to achieve.

- **Evaluate symptoms regularly**. Monitor the way the goals reduce mental h symptoms and improve the activeness and quality of life.

When thinking about goal setting, it is important to think about the things in life that you enjoy or value. The concept behind goal setting in CBT is that you are working towards something that will enhance your mood, assist you to connect with the things which are important to you and award you for the efforts you have put in. So, instead of thinking about goals that might be a result of self-critical thinking, start to think about things that are significant to you.

Once you have a hint about your goal and what you want to achieve, it is good to make sure that is specific. If you have a specific goal, it will guide you to know exactly what you need to do, and for how long you might need to spend doing it. This way, you can tell when you have accomplished your goal.

Your therapist can help you set goals and work towards making it a reality, but if you already developed an idea about the goals you wanted to work towards, this will help you to set the ball rolling.

Life Style Changes

Is your life packed with so many things to do and too little time? Are you the kind of person who takes dinner at the nearest restaurant before you go home? Do you experience sleepless nights? If you are living a life where you are eating a poor diet, doing limited exercise or one where you don't get enough sleep, perhaps it is why you are feeling depressed.

This section will take you through three quality strategies to calm your life. We shall further help you rediscover the enthusiasm for getting back to doing those morning exercises every day.

Designing Calming diets

Why you need to eat healthily

Everybody needs to make a choice to improve their diet. We consider a person to be eating a healthy meal if it has all the nutrients. Most people don't know that eating a balanced diet has many advantages. Some of the benefits that you get when you choose to eat a meal that contains all nutrients include reducing the chances of getting obesity

Many people across the world like foods that have a higher percentage of calories. This is not recommended at all. In fact, if your level of calories intake is higher than the rate at which your body is burning calories, you have a higher chance to add a lot of weight. So, you need to make sure that you consume calories depending on the level of activeness of your body.

Another important thing to consider when you aim to eat a balanced diet, make sure you don't just eat a meal which has three types of nutrients. Instead, eat a complete meal which will provide your body with all the nutrients that you deserve.

At times, if your moods are not ok you may get tempted to eat excessively. This often happens with the ladies. Some even decide to eat foods which contain high amounts of sugar and fat.

But, did you know that eating for the sake of your emotions doesn't last for a long time? Most of the time it only lasts for an hour or so. The long-term effect of having a poor diet is that you become much depressed.

Go for the little portion

Nowadays, the amount of food that people tend to eat has increased in size. Many people eat much compared to the people who lived before us. If you are among those people who can't just eat the right amount of food. You can use the following tips to improve yourself.

- **Get a smaller plate.** Sometimes all it takes for you to eat the right size is to buy a small plate. Using a smaller plate makes your mind to think that you have eaten a lot.

- **Don't eat fast.** It is always recommended for one to eat slowly. This gives more time for your stomach and the brain to communicate when you need to stop eating.

- **Serve food once.** When it comes to eating, just serve yourself once and keep away the dishes with the remaining food. This trick prevents you from wanting to serve yourself food again.

- **Eating in a restaurant**. Remember that the meals in a restaurant are twice the normal meals we take daily. This means that you should not eat all the meal yourself. If you are seated in the restaurant with a friend, you can allocate him or her some of it.

Adopt a nutrition formula

There are people who opt to eat several types of food such as French fries and ketchup to enhance their low moods. One of the reasons for this is because these foods are rich in carbohydrates. Their body has a good mechanism to transform the carbohydrates into sugar and consume it. This fast rate of food conversion results in a rapid drop of blood sugar. The resulting effect includes an increase in sugar cravings.

So, instead of eating foods which have carbohydrates, one should go for foods rich in fiber and carbs so that they can boost the levels of blood sugar. Complex carbs exist in vegetables, whole grains, and legumes.

Never skip breakfast

Breakfast has been considered by many to be the most essential meal that every human being should ensure that they don't miss. By just eating breakfast, you can control your weight. Whole meal cereal is recommended since it is a nutritious diet to start your day.

Take five portions of fruit and vegetables

You should aim to consume a minimum of five fruits every day. Other diets like fruit juice without sugar and vegetables added to meals play a role. Include a fruit in each of your breakfasts if you want to make sure you are taking a healthy meal.

Eat a lot of fish

Try to eat two portions of fish every week. Fish is very rich in proteins, vitamins as well as minerals which contribute to your overall health. Only salmon, sardines, fresh tuna, and mackerel are rich in the omega-3 fats. Omega-3 fats are beneficial to the body, besides preventing complex problems related to the heart, they help cure other related diseases.

Include starch diet

Certain types of foods such as rice, cereals, potatoes and many others contribute to a large percentage of your diet. It is a good practice to have this diet into your meal. You should not forget to add whole grain to your diet also. Whole grain is foods which have a higher percentage of fiber.

Reduce the intake of sugar and fat

To stay healthy, make sure you eliminate saturated fats from your list. Foods rich in saturated fats are dangerous to your body. They are among the leading causes of heart disease. If you can purchase vegetable oil, go for it. Eat lean meat. Instead of buying foods which contain higher amounts of fat, buy avocados and oily fish which are free from unsaturated fats.

Reduce your levels of sugar consumption

If there is one thing which you need to pay much attention is taking drinks with a high concentration of sugar. These drinks are some of the factors which will make you add in weight. Instead of taking processed drinks, eat foods which have natural sugar.

Reduce the levels of salt consumption

Excessive consumption of salt is dangerous to your body; it might lead to blood pressure. Limit the amount of salt that you put in your food. Another way you can ensure that you don't take much salt is to avoid eating processed foods. Always make sure you read the food labels to note down the level of salt. Don't forget that food such as bacon and cheese contain a higher percentage of salt. However, many people don't take time to consider this fact.

Family and friends

Our family members can help us a lot to cope with our anxiety and fear. They can be there to do what they can to offer us guidance, listen to some of the issues we go through and many more. On the other hand, they can also make us want to run away and hide because of some of the demands they present to us.

Sometimes they complain about problems which they are the authors of the same problems, leaving you feeling depressed and tired. In this section, we will look at the merits and drawbacks of having people in your life and some of the ways in which you can benefit from their relationships. Remaining connected to others.

Remaining connected to others

As much as friends and our close relatives can stress us, many studies still support the role that a good family relationship does in improving the overall state of a person. To stay connected with your family friends relieves the mental state of an individual. Good relationship reduces mental stress.

Therefore, any time you seem to be worried or even depressed, getting in touch with your close friends can help you fight stress. Speaking with the people you love helps relieve pain and negative thoughts about life. Some of the tips you can apply include:

- Meeting physically with your friends is a sure way of staying connected.

- Eat together with your close family members. Make jokes and have fun.

- Volunteer to help your community or school

- Look for the phone numbers of those friends whom you haven't spoken for a while and call them.

- Walk around your neighborhood and make new friends. Get to know the people whom you share similar values.

- Volunteer to help your relatives who may be having problems. You can clean their compound if it is dirty.

From the above tips, to stay in touch with your friends does not need you to spend a lot of money. All you need to set a side is the time and effort. This effort will benefit both you and the people you visit.

However, most people who are going through social anxiety might experience a big problem when dealing with this issue. But, you only need to start small. Get in touch with one person, it could be your brother, cousin or even your long time classmate. If you are that person who believes you can't get time to interact with your family friends. The next section will help you discover ways in which you can set time.

Allocate designated time for interaction

Many people who suffer from anxiety are never secure when they delegate any task to someone else. They believe that without any of their efforts, the end result will fall short of their required standards. I guess this has ever happened to you one time. But, what should you do when you are depressed to the point where you cannot perform your duties. Whether you like it or not, you will need to learn how to assign some tasks for people to help you. If you struggle to deliver when you are under a lot of stress, chances are that you are going to mess up everything. Besides that, your level of anxiety is going to increase. So, assigning some tasks to your friends to help you always solve the problem.

Here are tips to read when you want to delegate your tasks:

- Trust your partner to help you in some of the duties at home

- Hire a rental service to come and help in cleaning your compound.

- Spend some time let's say on a Sunday to prepare a meal which you can eat the next week.

- Ensure that you enroll in online banking. This will help you save the time of travelling to the bank to pay your monthly bills.

- Speak to one of your family members so that he or she can participate in a communal cleaning service.

As you can see, it is very simple to delegate some of the tasks. You don't need to do it yourself. All you need to do is to be confident and hopeful that you the person you have requested to step in for you will do an excellent job. In addition, some of these ideas may require you to cash in some money. For instance, if you want to hire a rental cleaning company, you will need to pay the company some fees for the services. You may look at this as a costly idea, but in the long run, it is worthy because you will get time to rest.

When it comes to assigning tasks, it is also good if you can give some guidance to the person so that they do a wonderful job. Delegating some of your tasks will relieve you from the burdens of life that you are going through. This then helps reduce stress and depression.

Teach yourself to say no

Most people who are anxious don't know when to say no. Majority of the times they find themselves accepting to perform a given task whenever requested. Anxiety is never a good feeling; it prevents an individual from disclosing their real feelings. Whenever this happens, the end result is anger and frustration. Plus, if you don't learn to resist certain requests, there are people who will take advantage of your situation. This means you are going to get overworked.

So, if you would like to handle this situation, you need to first identify scenarios which you always accept requests when it is not from your own heart. It could be happening while you are at work, with your family friends or even when you are in a new environment. The next time people ask you to do them a favor or something which you are not comfortable. Follow these steps:

Think about the request. For example, if John is going to ask you to buy for him a bottle of soda while you are coming to work, you tell him like this, "I understand that it would be more convenient for you if I bought for you the bottle of soda". The trick with this move is that you will get time to think about the request.

Maintain an eye contact with the person once you have said no.

Tell John a short reason why you aren't going to do so.

Remember, once you respond by saying no. You may upset the individual. So, try to be gentle. Don't overreact.

This is the reason why you should make gum your new friend

Stressed? Overwhelmed with anxiety? Research recommends chewing a piece of chewing gum. And not only does it get rid of stress, but research shows that chewing gum intensifies the flow of blood to the brain and makes a person stay alert. Well, that is something to cheer or chew.

For many years, human beings have been searching for something to chew. The ancient Mayans and Greeks relied on tree resin, while the first "chewing gum" was created in the 1800s from chicle. Although today's gum tastes much better, the ancient Mayans and Greeks could have been searching for something. The studies indicate that the early chewers might have experienced less stress compared to those who did not chew gum.

Chewing gum is related to reduced anxiety and decreased levels of cortisol. The stress relief can happen immediately but has a long-term effect also. In one particular study, participants who were tasked to chew gum twice a day for fourteen days ranked their anxiety to be significantly lower compared to the non-chewers. Furthermore, the gum chewers not only feel less stressed but they also become more alert. In another research, participants who chewed gum and at the same time assigned to finish memory tasks had quick response time and higher levels of attention span compared to the non-chewers.

It is correct that chewing gum helps deal with anxiety, but how does that work? It may not be the chewing of gum that does the jinx, in a particular study, people who were instructed to pretend they are chewing gum didn't experience the same effects. While it is still unknown why chewing gum helps relieve stress, it may have to do with the flavor. Research recommends that flavored gum increases brain arousal as opposed to the standard gum. Chewing of gum can further activate the senses because of the smell, touch, and taste, which might explain why it has been found to improve mood and increase the level of alertness.

If you want to start to chew gum as means to reduce anxiety, make sure you pick the sugar-free gum. It contains fewer calories. Plus, it has been found to help reduce teeth cavities and clean teeth.

Chapter 3:
Face Your fears, anxiety, depression, and Worry

Anxiety Disorders-Therapy

If you are a common victim of panic attacks, worries, and obsessive thoughts, you could be disturbed by anxiety disorders. However, you don't need to live with fear and anxiety. Getting some treatment might benefit you. In fact, for most people who have been found to experience anxiety disorder, therapy has been considered the most effective treatment. Therapists can train you to learn how to manage your worries and anxiety levels, and overcome your fears.

Therapy as a treatment for anxiety disorder

Research has proven that therapy is the most effective option for treating anxiety disorders. The reason for this is anxiety therapy treats more than the symptoms of the problem. Therapy can help you rediscover the hidden causes of your fears and worries; discover the best way to relax; look at situations in a different perspective, and discover better problem-solving skills. Therapy provides you the tools to deal with anxiety and trains you how to use them.

Anxiety disorders are not the same, that means therapy should be customized to your exact symptoms and diagnosis. For example, if you are found to have OCD, you will have a different type of treatment from an individual who wants a solution to anxiety. The length of the therapy will further depend on how severe the condition is. However, the majority of anxiety therapies are short-term. Different types of therapies are designed to treat different conditions related to anxiety. However, the best methods are:

- Exposure therapy
- Cognitive behavioral therapy

Each of the anxiety therapies might be used alone or integrated with other forms of therapy.

Anxiety therapy could be applied privately or in a group.

CBT for Anxiety

CBT is a popular type of therapy known for treating anxiety conditions. Studies have been done and reported CBT to be the best treatment favorable for phobias, anxiety disorder, panic disorder and many others. CBT is designed to handle negative thought patterns. It has two components involved:

Cognitive therapy assesses the way negative thoughts contribute to anxiety.

Behavior therapy assesses how an individual behaves and react in conditions that cause anxiety.

The foundation of CBT lies in the thoughts. This is because our thoughts affect how we feel and not the state which you are going through. For instance, if your friend calls you and invites you to go and attend their birthday party. Here are some of the possible ways that you can think about the birthday invitation.

Thought#1: The party looks fun. I like to go out and make new friends.

Emotions: Excited, happy.

Thought#2: Parties are never something I enjoy going to. I'd rather stay in doors and watch some comedy.

Emotions: Neutral.

Thought#3: I don't know what to do and say at parties. I will look dejected if I go.

Emotions: Sad, anxious.

The above example shows that the same event can result in different emotions among different people. It takes us back to our expectations, attitudes, and beliefs. For the individuals who experience negative thinking, anxiety disorder, all stimulate the destructive emotions of anxiety and fear. The end goal of CBT for anxiety is to recognize and rectify these negative beliefs and thoughts. The slogan is that if you can find a way to change your mode of thinking, then it is possible to change how you feel.

Chapter 3: Face Your fears, anxiety, depression, and Worry

CBT for Challenging your thoughts and Anxiety

Thought challenging refers to the ways in which you can change the negative thinking patterns which cause anxiety. You replace them with more realistic and positive thoughts. It has three steps:

1. **Recognize the negative thoughts.** When you have an anxiety disorder, situations are seen to be more dangerous than they are.

2. **Test your negative thoughts.** Here, your therapist will help you measure the level of anxiety-triggering beliefs. This involves questioning the evidence and assessing the truth of your negative expectations. Some of the methods which you can borrow and apply in this process include weighing the pros and cons and analyzing the alternatives of what you are anxious about happening.

3. **Substitute negative thoughts with convincing thoughts.** Once you have identified irrational predictions, it is now

time to override them with new positive beliefs. Your therapist can further offer assistance in the way you build realistic statements about yourself.

To better develop a clear picture on how thought challenging operates in CBT, here is an example: Joyce can't pass close to the passageway because she's terrified she will fall, and then everyone would assume she's wild. Joyce's therapist has asked her to list down negative beliefs, highlight the gaps in her way of thinking and create a rational explanation. Below are the results.

Negative thought 1: If it happens that I collapse while on the passageway.

Cognitive alteration: The worst prediction

A truthful thought: I have never fainted, so it's rare that I may pass out on the passageway.

Negative thought 2: If I am going to pass out, it will be disgusting.

Cognitive distortion: Blowing things beyond the limit

A realistic thought: If I faint; I will recover in a few minutes. That will not be disgusting.

Negative thought 3: People are going to look at me as a crazy person.

Cognitive distortion: Jumped to a conclusion.

A realistic thought: People are going to be concerned whether I am fine.

Switching negative thoughts with accurate ones might look like something easy to do, however, it is still difficult. Why? Negative thoughts originate from a long-term thinking pattern. It requires enough practice to break this habit. That's why CBT also has personal practice. CBT can also include:

Learning to notice when you're feeling anxious and how that feels in the body.

Learning some coping skills and techniques to relax to help you overcome panic and anxiety.

Resisting your worries in practical life

Exposure therapy-anxiety

Anxiety is not a great feeling; therefore, you should avoid it if you can. A common practice which many people adopt is evading the situations which make them appear anxious. If you are petrified by tall heights, you could decide to change your route so that you don't pass near a tall height. Or if you don't like giving a public speech. Let's say that giving a public speech makes you shiver; you might decide to speak to one of your friends who is familiar or loves giving a public speech to go speak on your behalf.

However, this approach of avoiding meeting your real fear creates so much inconvenience. Besides, you will never get the right chance to fight your fears. In fact, evading your fears strengthens them.

Chapter 3: Face Your fears, anxiety, depression, and Worry

Exposure therapy brings you face to face with the objects or situations you fear. The unique idea behind exposure therapy is that it makes you interact several times with your fears to the point where you gain total control over them. You attain a point of no more anxiety. The exposure is achieved in either one or two ways. A therapist will ask you to imagine dreadful states or you could simply interact with them in reality. With exposure therapy, you can integrate it with CBT or use it alone.

Systematic desensitization

Rather than meeting your terrifying situation immediately, systematic desensitization will allow you to slowly question your fears, cultivate confidence, and learn the skills for controlling panic. This approach has three parts:

Mastering the relaxation skills. In this part, the therapist guides you through several techniques like relaxing your muscles and taking a deep breath. You will then perform it in therapy and when you're at home on your own. Now, when you start to learn how to overcome your fears, you will frequently use the above learned techniques to reduce your anxiety response.

Listing your fears. Next, you will develop a list of 10-20 scary situations that lead to your final goal. For instance, if your ultimate goal is to conquer the fear of snakes, you can begin by looking at snake photos and then visiting a national park where there are many snakes. Each step needs to be specific, with a measurable and clear objective.

Follow the steps: By following each instruction given to you by your therapist. You can slowly begin to attempt each of the things you have listed on the list. The main thing here is to face the fearful situation until you have total control over it. This way, you'll realize that the feelings don't hurt and they vanish. Each time the anxiety becomes intense, you'll shift to the relaxation technique you have been taught. The moment you have relaxed enough; you can take back your focus to the same situation. You will need to go through the steps until you don't experience any fear.

Complementary therapies tailored for anxiety disorders

While you are busy trying to fight anxiety disorder, you could also attempt some complementary therapies designed to help reduce stress levels and allow you to attain the correct emotional balance.

Exercise. It is a natural anxiety reliever and stress buster. Studies have shown that 30 minutes of exercise 3-5 times a week can significantly relieve anxiety. To realize the required benefits, it is important to set aside one hour to perform aerobic exercise.

Relaxation methods such as mindfulness, meditation, when done every day, will help heal anxiety and boost the emotional well-being of an individual.

Biofeedback. This comes with inbuilt sensors which help monitor physiological functions like breathing rate, heart rate, and muscle tension. This will help an individual to notice the anxiety response of the body and learn how to manage it by following the correct relaxation mechanisms.

Hypnosis. Sometimes it is used together with CBT for anxiety. When you are relaxing, the therapist can use several techniques to assist you in combatting your fears.

How to make anxiety therapy work?

It is hard to find a quick solution for anxiety. Combating an anxiety disorder needs time and dedication. Therapy consists of fighting your fears instead of evading them The most important thing to do is to continue with the treatment and adhere to the advice of your therapist. If you happen to feel disappointed with the rate of recovery, remember what I said at the start about therapy-it is the best treatment for anxiety. Remain patient. You will see the benefits if you stick to them to the end.

You can still treat your anxiety problems by remaining positive. Think positive and make positive choices. Remember that, everything you do has an impact on your anxiety. So, you need to set the pathway for success by making positive decisions. Positive decisions will improve your level of relaxation.

Try to study about anxiety. Combating anxiety requires many external factors. You can't just sit and wait to fight anxiety if you are not ready to find out more about your problem. Education is a key factor. While it may not treat anxiety, by virtue of you reading a few articles here and there you gain the positive feeling that anxiety can be cured.

Expand your network. Loneliness and isolation are triggering factors for anxiety. Reduce your vulnerability by meeting people. Form a habit to visit friends; join a support group; share your concerns and fears with a trusted friend.

Adopt a healthy exercise habit. Studies have shown that there is a relationship between physical activity and anxiety. This means then that you need to have time to go to the gym and work out. Don't take alcohol and stimulants as a means to treat your problem. That could just worsen the situation.

Reduce stress. List some of the things which you think are contributing to you feeling stressed. Figure out how you can handle it. Avoid sitting around people who will make you feel anxious, say no to extra tasks or responsibilities. Set aside time for relaxation and fun in your daily routine.

5 Sure-fire ways to combat fear and anxiety

If you discover that you are feeling more anxious. Here are some of the things you can do.

1. Breathing

Perhaps, you have read how you can make use of breathing to overcome anxiety.

This is worth reading also:

Breathing quickly and shallowly will help trigger other anxiety related symptoms. This means if you can manage your rate of breathing, you will succeed in stopping other symptoms of anxiety. When you feel anxious, this is what you should do:

- Stop everything you are doing.
- Pay attention to your breath

- Take a deep breath
- Then begin to breath out slowly

If you can giving it a try, you will discover how magical it is at overcoming anxiety. The most crucial thing is to breath out several times.

That sounds good. But, when you get anxious chances are that you may forget everything and all the good advice escapes through the window. This brings us to the next point.

2. Get ready

If you know that you are overwhelmed by fear and anxiety by some of the things you are about to do, such as a speech or anything that is making you shiver, you'll discover that even by thinking about it for a few seconds, you will start to experience anxiety. The end result of this effect is your whole body becomes more anxious. But, you will come to realize that the technique of breathing while thinking about your scariest situation helps you fight the anxiety. This gives you peace of mind when the actual event arrives.

One particular symptom of excessive fear or anxiety is to fail to think correctly. This happens because the emotional part of your brain overrides the analytical brain. But, in the present situation, we want to maintain a clear thought. And making sure that your brain is working clearly will help you to relax.

3. Use a different part of your brain

If you are overcome by fear, it can be difficult to think straight. But, if we can train our minds to make use of specific parts of the brain, it can be a wonderful solution in relaxing our emotions.

The simple way to achieve this has to do with numbers. You can rate your own fear on a scale of 1-10 where 10 is most fearful and 1 being fully relaxed. When feelings of anxiety strike you, figure out the number on the scale where you are. Are you on a 7 or 5? If you can do this, it will help fight the anxiety because it restarts the thinking brain, relieving the emotion and making you feel relaxed.

I remember when I was a student and was asked to give a public speech to over two hundred students. I felt very anxious before I opened my mouth to speak. But, knowing this technique, I was able to apply it, when my level of anxiety dropped to 2, I started to give the speech. It turned out to be an amazing speech and everybody applauded me. I was able to control my anxiety with this simple technique.

4. Control your imagination

Fear and anxiety are at their best whenever we start to think of the worst situations in life.

We imagine so that we can see the future and plan ahead. However, some people imagine only negative things. I don't mean a little bit of negative imagination is bad. No! The problem comes in when everything we imagine is negative. There is not a single positive. And this is the major problem that leads to fear and anxiety.

Some people negatively use their imagination and end up suffering from more anxiety compared to those who use it constructively. Anxious people and chronic worriers seem to exploit their imaginations to the point where upcoming events look catastrophic. No wonder their entire lives are filled with anxiety and fear.

Some people might not be aware that they are doing this. Here is a solution for you:

- Find a chair, sit and do some breathing in and out.

- Count from a specific number until your scale reads 1-2

- Allow yourself to be in the situation that is fearful, but look composed, relaxed and calm at the same time.

5. Adopt the AWARE technique

AWARE is an abbreviation which stands for:

A: Accepting the anxiety. Don't attempt to fight it.

W: Watch the anxiety. Simply watch it and when you can identify it, narrow down your level of fear and begin to breath longer on the out-breath.

A: Act normally. Just go on talking or doing what you were doing as if nothing has happened. This sends a dominant signal to your idle mind whose response is not required because nothing abnormal is taking place.

R: Repeat the highlighted steps in your mind when necessary.

E: Expect the best. One of the best feelings in life is when you discover that you can manage fear better than you thought possible.

Overcoming anxiety and fear will help you get the extra space in life to concentrate on what you want to do. It takes dedication and effort but just picture the rewards.

Chapter 4:
Mindful Acceptance

Have you ever felt anxious, stressed, or simply overwhelmed by life?

We live in a world with so many things to do. With texts and emails flying all around, you probably get stressed out every day. Fortunately, there is a wonderful habit that you can apply to help relax and appreciate life. We call it mindfulness.

Mindfulness is the process of putting all your attention on the present moment and accepting it without any question. This is an amazing place to start if you are searching for the major factor in happiness. If you can follow the correct steps, mindfulness will heal problems related to anxiety and stress. This will also help an individual to appreciate the little moments as they emerge. Living in a world where there is much madness and chaos, practicing mindfulness could present the best healing.

Practice Mindfulness

1. Allocate time and space to practice mindfulness

You want the time you allocate for mindfulness to be calm, quiet, and comforting. You will also prefer to select a time when you are unlikely to get disrupted. Find a peaceful and comfortable space that you can relax while you will be performing mindfulness. Let this space be specifically for practicing mindfulness. Not for something else. This will help notify your body any time you sit down to begin to calm down.

2. Focus on the current moment

Don't think about anything else. Allow your mind to remain in the present. Forget about the past or the future. This is the time to focus only on the present situation. Always return to concentrate on your breath and listen to the sounds near you.

3. Free yourself and don't do anything but be yourself.

You don't need to be running around all the time to get things done. There are times that your body wants to recharge for you to become productive. This is the moment that you can realize it. Let your mind enjoy this rest while you think of it as a way of living a good life in the long-term.

4. Avoid thinking of the past. Don't plan for the future. Don't stare at the time.

You know well that the past is gone. And you can't reverse the past. Well, why can't you forget about it? Or let it go? Stop thinking about anything that has already taken place. Don't even think of what is going to happen. Focus on the present moment without feeling worried about anything. Don't be worried about time or a task that you haven't completed.

5. Focus on your thoughts, actions, words, and motivations.

When you begin to think, say or do something, ask yourself what is the premise behind it?

6. Recognize your judgements and let them go.

It is fine to have judgements. This is something normal that everyone goes through. However, it crucial to understand them and let them disappear. Judgements are never permanent, and there is time for your mind to change, so don't get obsessed about your previous judgments.

7. Return to the present moment

If the feelings of anxiousness begin to come or you start to regret a mistake you made in the past, shift your attention back to the present moment. Tell yourself that you have no power to change anything. If it has happened, you can't reverse it.

8. Avoid being hard on yourself

Your mind will wander a bit while you are in the process of practicing mindfulness. You might begin to remember the days that you were a young boy, or even how you used to enjoy going to school while you were young. It is normal. Everyone's mind wanders a bit while they are practicing mindful meditation. So don't be too hard on yourself. Let that passing thought vanish, take a long breath and reset your focus.

Chapter 4: Mindful Acceptance

How to practice Mindfulness Meditation?

Mindfulness and meditation come with different benefits which are both mental and physical. However, most people don't recognize that the two are different things. Mindfulness is just one form of meditation.

Most people think that meditation has an instant effect, they have this belief that something is supposed to happen immediately. Some think that mediation will empty their minds and allow them to stay at peace in a split second. Others think that they should feel weightless.

Meditation and mindfulness, what is the difference?

To clear the doubt, mindfulness involves being alert. You can practice mindfulness at any time of the day. For example, you can practice it while having a small talk with your close relative.

Mindfulness meditation refers to a well-known type of meditation among the Buddhists. If you are interested in integrating the two into a single mindful meditation, here are the steps.

1. Allocate time to practice

No need to have a fixed time. But, if you can set something to alert you like an alarm or even develop a certain habit, it will trigger your body to assume the state of meditation.

2. Find a place which is free of disturbances

It could be a room where nobody passes or comes in. As long as you ensure that the place is silent and has no interruptions.

3. Relax yourself

Get a position which will allow you to feel comfortable. It can be a seat or a mat. Remember, sitting down while meditating is the best way to go. You can decide to sit, stand or kneel. The choice is up to you to decide. But, make sure that you don't have tight clothes on which can prevent you from breathing freely.

4. Now, concentrate on the movements of your legs

5. Sit straight, but remain relaxed

Let your backbone take its normal curve. Comfort is very important here.

6. Your arms should be loose

Now, loose your hands while you bend your elbow slowly. Your upper arms should be in parallel with your upper body; and place your palms whenever it feels comfortable.

7. Relax your gaze

Let your chin go down and permit your eyelids to move downward. No need to close your eyes. Just stare at anything that crosses your eyes.

8. Relax your whole body

You can begin with your toes until you are completely relaxed with the whole body. But, don't forget your shoulders, jaw, face etc.

9. Spend some time to think about your intention.

This should not take long. Start with simple details for performing mindfulness, and your defined goals. You might want to feel energized for the entire day, or you might aim to reduce the amount of judgement which bothers you often on a regular basis.

10. Pay attention to your breath

Take some 8-20 seconds to think about the air which you breathe in, how it flows through your breathing system. Think about the good feeling you experience when you breath in and breath out.

11. Recognize when your mind starts to wander

This is fine, but you don't want to force away any passive beliefs. When you find your mind starting to wander, slowly return it to breathing.

12. Excuse your wandering mind

Sometimes, your mind might begin to wander every now and then. In this case, don't fight it. Just stop and watch it as it wanders.

13. When you are through, raise your gaze gently

Just remember, meditation has no perfect time. You can meditate in the morning, afternoon or evening. There are no limits for how long one can meditate. However, if it is your first time, we recommend letting your sessions last for about 10 minutes.

14. **Gently bring your focus to the present moment**

Take time to rise up and be careful to spot any sounds which are in your environment. Think for a moment the way your body feels in the present moment, right from top to bottom. Think about your emotions and feelings.

There are times when you need to apply mindfulness in specific scenarios.

Mindfulness-anxiety

By focusing on your breath, it will gives you a lot of benefits such as relieving your anxiety. Even though you might not be careful to monitor your process of breathing, if you could track your breathing, you will learn how to use it to relax.

If your level of apprehension begins to rise, the first thing that you are supposed to do is to pay attention to your level of breathing. Often, anxiety increases your rate of breathing in and out. This means that if you can pay attention to your breath and allow yourself to experience the flow of the air in the lungs and out of the lungs, you will relieve your anxiety.

Here are four things that you should pay attention to regarding the process of developing a focused culture of breathing.

1. Don't calm down so much to the point where you create a barrier for your breathing

Just sit upright and allow your lungs enough space to breath in oxygen. Identify regions of your body where you feel the tension and imagine that you are breathing air in to that region.

2. Make sure you breathe through the nose

While you can breathe through the mouth, the nose is the correct part of the body where all human beings should breath through. The nose has hair to filter the air and ensure that you only take in clean air. Plus, the nose moistens the air so that it is in the right condition for the body.

3. Practice abdominal breathing

Breath like you are directing all the air into your stomach. If you breath out, do so through your mouth gently and allow your stomach to return back to its normal position.

4. Know the difference between deep and shallow breathing

Shallow breathing will stop at the chest but abdominal breathing takes over your entire lungs. Plus, it will facilitate complete oxygen exchange.

Mindfulness is good if you aim at relieving your cognitive symptoms of depression. By concentrating in the present moment, it helps many individuals to recognize their negative thoughts. They also recognize that the negative thoughts exist without making any judgement, and they realize that those thoughts don't depict the reality. Furthermore, mindfulness will help individuals to discover their thoughts aren't that powerful and allow them to vanish fast.

If one can learn and understand the way they think rather than getting carried away by emotions of their own thoughts, it becomes very hard for them to be dragged down by any negative thinking. You develop total control of your thoughts. This way, when the thoughts come, you are able to manage them.

It is also good to develop a connection with mother nature when you are trying to fight depression. Set aside some time to bask in the sunshine, it can have a big impact on one's physical and mental well-being.

Nature is the best boost for your mental well-being. If you go to work in an office, spend a few moments to stare at nature. It will help boost your overall well-being. Notice and accept the situation when you feel scared or depressed. Think about how active your stress response is instead of how inadequate you are as an individual.

Practice writing a gratitude journal every night. Building a culture of gratitude is free, and it doesn't take a lot of time, but there is a possibility you'll get massive benefits from it.

The benefits of practicing mindfulness

The benefits of mindfulness and meditation are widely known in the scientific community. Here are some of the positive effects one gets by practicing mindfulness:

- **Reduction of stress.** Practicing mindfulness has proven to reduce the amount of cortisol in our bodies. Besides lowering our stress in the present, it also helps us reduce stress in the long-term and in response to future events.

- **More creativity**. Innovation and thinking creatively take place in the neocortex of the brain. For the neocortex to function correctly, we have to clear our mind of emotional thoughts. Mindfulness is the perfect medicine for doing this.

- **Improved health**. There are specific studies which have proven mindfulness can heal someone and increase emotional intelligence. Mindfulness makes people become compassionate.

- **Fights depression**.

The bottom line

Meditation is an amazing medicine for anxiety.

It goes beyond temporarily helping you relax. It goes into a deep level by changing the structure and function of your brain. Meditation reprograms your brain so that it becomes less anxious. Mindfulness meditation needs no special training and can bring anxiety relief in just 10 minutes a day.

Learning how to quiet your mind can be very challenging, however, guided meditation makes everything easy. It gives you the chance to apply knowledge and techniques from the best meditation experts.

Chapter 5:
Narrowing down your specific Worries

Containing your Worry

E ven though a little bit of worry is normal is the way every one of us was created, there are times when it can feel like we are worrying too much. Containing your worry is all about letting yourself worry no matter what happens, but only at the designated time of the day which you decide yourself.

The first thing you need to turn your focus to when containing your worry is uncertainty. This is the most common types of worry which a lot of people experience right from when you are a child. You are worried about what you are going to eat tomorrow. Some people are worried about how they are going to arrive at their places of work. If you realize that you are worrying about something whose end result is uncertain, soon you will start feeling overwhelmed that you have no control over the situation. And this can have a negative impact on the rest of your life. Most of these worries begin with what if...?

Alternatively, there are some things which we worry about but we don't know that we can solve them here and now. So, when we narrow down the worries, we look at practical worries which you have the ability to deal with and hypothetical worries which depend on uncertainty.

Face your Career Crisis and Financial Woes

Many people worry a lot about money. They are obsessed about their savings, home values, accounts, and promotions. More basic needs add a lot of worry. People are worriesd about losing their job, and the ability to provide the basic needs like clothing, shelter, and healthcare. Even though money is not more worthy than a person, we all need some amount of money to live.

Dealing with job anxieties

Nearly everyone is always worried about losing their job. You are not the only one. Even CEOs of top companies are always worried about the future of their company. An economic recession is something that will happen without any notice. It occurs spontaneously, and the results are catastrophic because millions of people can lose their jobs. It is very difficult to be sure whether a given career will continue to exist or it will be phased out. For example, there was a time when if you worked in a car manufacturing company, your job was considered safe.

These days, technology has been good and bad. It has increased the number of jobs in some sectors while reducing jobs in other sectors.

Change the look of your resume

One of best ways that you can be sure to handle anxiety related to jobs is to make use of the market opportunities. Whether you already have a job or you have just landed your first job, having a good resume is a must. If you don't know how to make your resume nice, you can hire a professional resume writer who can help create an attractive resume for you.

I know someone might be asking, why should I hire a professional resume writer? Well, if you didn't know, updating a resume is not something easy, I have seen a lot of people feel anxious when they want to update or edit their resume. And don't forget that when you are anxious, most people evade doing that particular thing which makes them feel anxious. Now, this is the reason why I recommend that you look for a professional resume writing company to help you. Below are more suggestions which you can use:

- Develop a schedule of how you want to update your resume. Your schedule should be specific on what you want to achieve.

- After you have updated your resume, present it to your friends to give you some feedback about it.

- Don't procrastinate about anything. Procrastinating will only increase your level of anxiety.

Make sure that your resume is short and highlights your strengths in the best possible way. Include keywords in your resume. The

keywords should be related to the job you are
looking for.

Developing flexibility

It does not matter what you are going through or
what you have gone through. It could be that you
have lost your job today, or they have transferred
you to a different department. As long as you are
a flexible person, you will still overcome all the
challenges which you encounter on the way. One
of the unique things about people who are
flexible is their ability to deal with the challenges
that come on their way. Because they are highly
flexible, they don't give up but adjust their
situations in accordance with the challenges.

I am talking about people who today are
discontinued from their job, but in the next
minute, they are already applying for new jobs.
Flexibility is key to realizing success and
overcoming some of the stress related to jobs.

While people who are not flexible will feel angry
and frustrated. Flexible people appreciate the
situation and figure out their next strategy.
Inflexible people will remain adamant about
change and resist making changes to their

previous choices, but this is not the same with flexible people. They always try something new, they are driven by the passion to achieve something different.

When you have this mental flexibility, you are strong enough to handle all the difficulties which you go through. You will know when to back off and when it is right to create a balance. Having a mental flexibility gives you the freedom to look at reality from a different angle.

A person with mental flexibility will understand that when change comes it is inevitable. This level of flexibility needs someone to be open to new experiences. One must know that truth is hard to tell.

Stable career

While people live an anxious life, it is understood that if your career is stable, you will not worry too much. One of the best things about ensuring that you don't worry so much is to develop a mechanism for handling the future. If you can increase your level of education. It is well and good. Education improves your level of knowledge and skills. This will make you a better person.

However, you need to also know that every career has its own problems. No career is stable. You could be laughing now, and then tomorrow crying.

Maintain your focus

If you are vulnerable to fear and anxiety, you will forever be controlled by fear. I say this because most people who are about to lose their jobs begin to think about so many negative things in their lives. These negative thoughts then ruin their lives.

I will suggest that if you are working, it is important to develop a culture of saving part of your income. If you can cultivate this culture. I am sure you will help reduce some of the fears and worries that you go through when you lose your job. Another thing which you need to do is to cut down on your expenses. If you can reduce your expenses, you will help save some income.

Dedicate yourself to a new strategy

If you can design a new strategy to use, it can help you stop worrying about your jobs and money. Can you imagine if you have a passive stream of income which at the end of every month you make a massive income? In this case, you know that even if you are going to lose your job, you will still manage to pay your monthly bills. And this gives you peace of mind.

Planning for the future

A few years ago, people used to work for over 40 years in a single company and look forward to living a better life later when they retire. Today, everything has changed. Pension plans have gone high.

While you may be right to be worried about not being able to enjoy your retirement years. If you can make use of the flexibility trait, you will be in a better state than that person who does not learn to be flexible. By being flexible, you will learn to handle the future while remaining composed. You will not be overwhelmed with fear or anxiety. By realizing that uncertainty has limits, you will begin to adapt to the different ways in which you can handle it.

Chapter 6:
Blue Print for Well-being

Transform the way you think and your attitude

At times, a lot of stress can lead to a thousand thoughts which are triggered by a little problem. But, the results are devastating. We get worked up sometime, and this irrational thought can lead to undue stress. However, with cognitive restructuring, you get to learn how you can control these kinds of thoughts and remain positive and realistic.

Cognitive restructuring is a behavioral technique related to cognitive therapy. This consists of learning how to change your way of thinking. Transform the wrong style of thinking and develop positive thinking.

How it works

There is nothing so frustrating than getting caught in a traffic jam while heading to work. Like many people, you perhaps get irritated, frustrated and angry. You might start to be worried about getting to work late or even failing to meet the deadlines of the day's tasks. These thoughts then give birth to stress.

You now have two choices: To let the stress destroy you until you lose your job or transform your way of thinking.

Cognitive restructuring focuses on thoughts, identifies when the thoughts are irrational, and lets you learn how to replace the thoughts and behaviors. Taking the example of the traffic scenario, think about rational situations. Does that situation lead you to feel stressed? Remember, this is a situation in which there's nothing that you can do to help you arrive early at your job. You can't step out of the vehicle and walk to your destination. It is, therefore, irrational to begin to imagine terrible things that might never happen. Rather than imagining those negative scenarios, focus your energy on the way you can evade getting caught in traffic the next time and stay away from stress.

This is how you can change your thoughts

Start by evaluating your fears and thoughts and find out whether they are rational or irrational.

You can ask yourself the following questions about your fears and thoughts.

- What is the worst possible result for this scenario?

- Can it harm me or any of my family?

- Am I assessing this situation in the right way and what proof do I have for my fears

- What effort or step can I do to change the situation

Begin by writing down on a sheet of paper your thoughts and highlight some of the facts that you know. Re-evaluate the facts, and create a comparison with your fears and thoughts, and figure out which one is rational.

It is possible to change your own thinking habits by yourself, but not many people can do that. Some people have the ability to learn new ways of thinking with the help of their processing ability and observation skills. For some, it does not occur quickly and they may need the help of a good therapist.

Develop a strong personal control

The weight on personal control is enormous. People who are not affected by depression or stress direct their energy to matters over which they have control but not things which are beyond their, limits.

Break bad habits

Fear can drive us to the point where we recognize and recall all our negative thoughts, this then makes us create the image in our mind where we view the world as a terrifying place to live. However, we can put an end to this trend by deliberately identifying the positive aspects and feeling joy we experience when we get in touch with someone who we love.

According to research done by Barbara Fredrickson it was discovered that positivity broadens our perspective. We have a wider view that gives us more options. And the more times we apply positivity, the more it builds, developing a resilience which permits us to function even in the hard times.

Get support

Fear can make us feel disconnected from the rest of our close friends. Finding support could be the best thing to help you become your normal self. Having friends and family members stay close to us can help us develop a sense of security. When we feel secure we become confident to deal with other related issues in life.

Different ways to help you come out of your fears

We all experience fears, anxieties and phobias. Sometimes we close our eyes and hold our breath while we ride the elevator to the 12th floor of an office building, while others just avoid going to the funeral because of the fear of seeing a coffin. Well, here are four different strategies which you can apply.

1. Focus on what is right before you

This is true of many things. If we can maintain our focus on what is right before our eyes, we have good chance to remain relaxed. This applies also when you find yourself in the midst of a stressful scenario.

2. Keep your cheerleaders close

Overcoming your fears is simple when you are in the company of your cheerleaders or friends. This is true whether you decide to challenge yourself to run a marathon or give a public speech.

3. Pay attention to your breath

Breathe in and breathe out but make sure that breathing out takes longer than breathing in. When you breathe in deeply, you activate your vagus nerve, which runs from your medulla oblongata situated in the brain stem, to the stomach. The long nerve connects the main nervous coordination and your central nervous system. It is often considered the link between our conscious and subconscious minds.

4. Apply some humor

Some jokes can help you feel relaxed and control the situation.

In summary, to face your fears and anxieties you need to stand strong. Identify some of the ways of developing personal control in your life.

1. Practice stress reduction mechanism like mindfulness.

2. Shift your focus to the positive emotions in your daily life.

3. Work and identify meaning in your life

4. Get support from your friends.

Still, if you are threatened by fear, don't forget other areas of your life.

Conclusion

Thank for making it through to the end of this book, let's hope it was informative and able to provide you with all of the tools you need to achieve your goals whatever they may be.

Sometimes change can be terrifying. The lack of control and anxiety involved can be confusing and frustrating to everyone. We all need support from our friends and families at certain point in our lives, often when we are in the process of learning something new or changing circumstances that we are in.

Most of the things which we learn in life are terrifying; including learning how to drive a car, learn how to ride a bike, etc. Take, for instance, mastering how to swim. Many young adults and children are afraid of getting into the water. However, given the right instruction, support and guidance we can develop ways to overcome our fears and master the different stages involved. Similarly, panic disorder, anxiety, phobias, and depression are no different.

Cognitive Behavioral Therapy

If we can understand why we behave and believe the way we do, there are a lot of things which we can do that will help:

- To change those behaviors and beliefs

- Develop correct, positive feelings about our self.

- Develop the correct feelings of being confident and in control

Once we recognize that courage is not the lack of fear we are in a position to go forward. Some guidance and support is helpful, but there are times when it is very frightening. If we want to grow and become better individuals, we shouldn't let fear hold us back.

We might feel that our problem is unique and it needs specific help. Yet similar experiences lie at the heart of all these problems. They grow and expand in the same way and we are weakened in the same way.